AF597948
TO:
FROM:

Printed in the United States of America

ISBN: 979-8-88779-168-5 (hbk)
ISBN: 979-8-88779-169-2 (ePub)

Library of Congress Cataloging-in-Publication Data has been applied for.

THE BEST BATH EVER!

HOW GOD WASHES AWAY OUR SIN AND MAKES US BRAND NEW

Written by
PAUL TAUTGES

Illustrated by
INGRID SAWUBONA

IT'S FUN TO GET DIRTY SOMETIMES, ISN'T IT?
Picking blueberries . . .
Helping in the kitchen

Catching frogs . . .
Or dripping ice cream all over yourself on a hot summer day!
BUT...

SOMETIMES GETTING DIRTY IS NO FUN AT ALL.
Walking in sandy shoes . . .
Spilling your hot chocolate . . .

NO MATTER HOW YOU GET DIRTY, YOU NEED A GOOD BATH TO GET CLEANED UP!

God's Book, the holy Bible, tells the true story of a great man who needed a good washing. But not just on the outside. He needed God to make him clean on the inside.

THAT MAN, MY FRIEND, IS ME!

HI! I'M NAAMAN.

TRY SAYING IT:  NEIGHHH + [man] = NAAMAN

I was a mighty warrior—the commander of the army of Aram. Because I did not know the one true God, I attacked God's people, worshiped false gods, and brought sacrifices to idols.

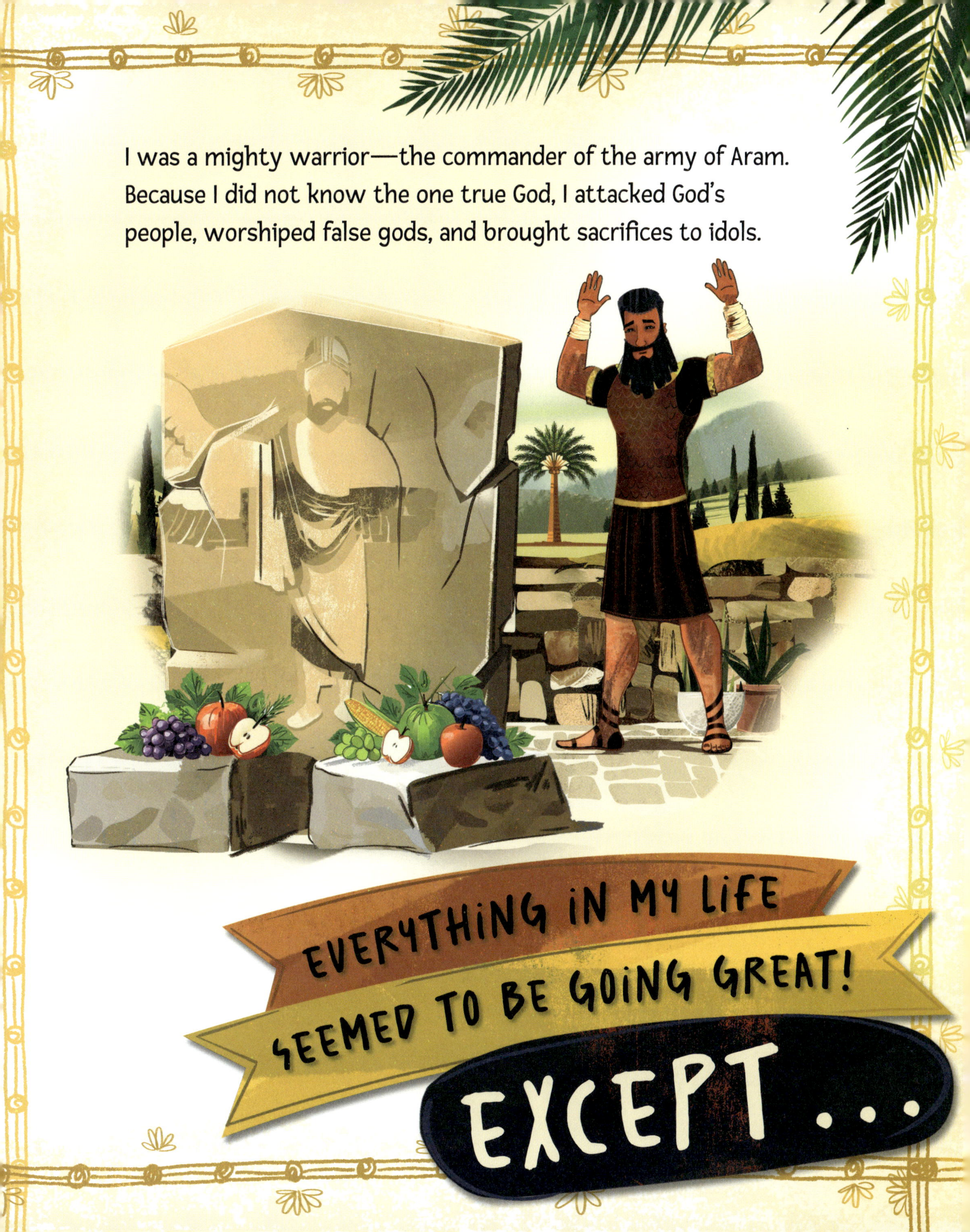

I HAD A BIG PROBLEM—
I WAS SICK WITH A
TERRIBLE SKIN DISEASE
CALLED LEPROSY.
IMAGINE BEING DIRTY AND
NEVER BEING ABLE TO GET
CLEAN. THAT WAS HOW I FELT.
NOTHING I DID COULD HEAL
MY SKIN OR MAKE ME FEEL BETTER!

But one day, a servant girl from Israel told my wife about a prophet who could heal me.
HIS NAME IS ELISHA, AND HE IS A MAN OF GOD!
THIS WAS WONDERFUL NEWS!

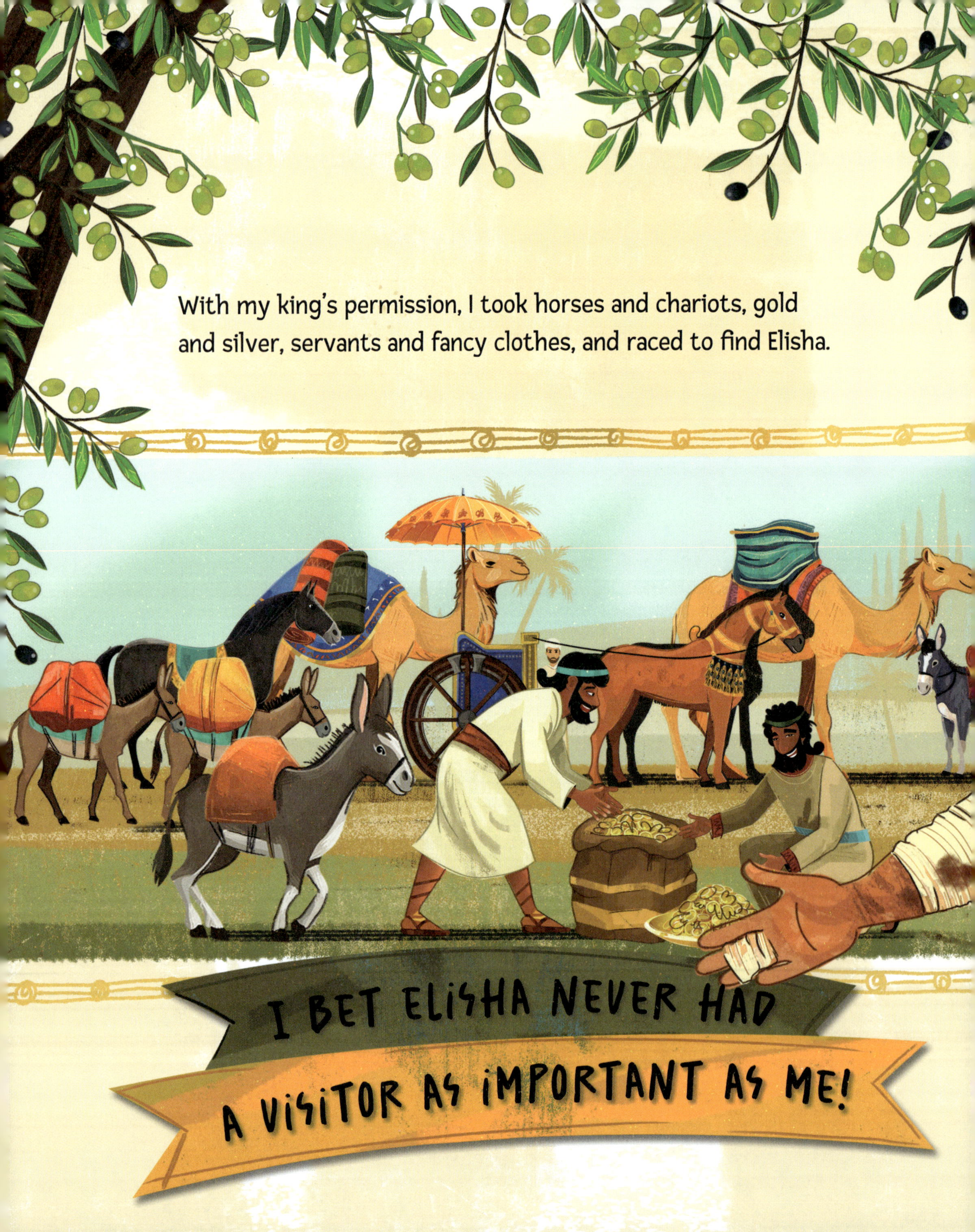
With my king's permission, I took horses and chariots, gold and silver, servants and fancy clothes, and raced to find Elisha.
I BET ELISHA NEVER HAD
A VISITOR AS IMPORTANT AS ME!

But he didn't even come out of his house!
Instead, he sent a servant to tell me,
ELISHA SAYS GOD WANTS YOU TO WASH YOURSELF IN THE JORDAN RIVER SEVEN TIMES, AND YOUR SKIN WILL BE HEALED.
WAIT . . .

WHAT?
ELISHA SHOULD COME TO ME, SAY A FANCY PRAYER, WAVE HIS HAND, AND CURE ME!
AND WHY SHOULD I HAVE TO TAKE A BATH IN THE MUDDY JORDAN RIVER? WE HAVE WAY BETTER RIVERS IN MY COUNTRY!
ELISHA HAD THIS TOTALLY WRONG!
I was so mad, I stomped back down the road.

But my servants stopped me!
Why can't he just heal me MY way?
SIR, IF THE PROPHET HAD ASKED YOU TO DO SOMETHING BRAVE, YOU WOULDN'T HAVE HESITATED!
IF GOD TELLS YOU TO WASH IN THE JORDAN, WHY NOT DO THAT?

They had a point.

I went down and dipped myself in the river seven times—

AND . . .

DO YOU KNOW WHAT HAPPENED NEXT?

GOD WASHED ME TOTALLY CLEAN!

MY SKIN BECAME AS GOOD AS NEW—
LIKE IT WAS WHEN I WAS A YOUNG BOY.
I WAS OVER-THE-MOON,
JUMP-FOR-JOY HAPPY!

My servants and I hurried back to Elisha's house, and this time Elisha came out to greet me.

I wanted to repay the prophet, so I begged him to take my gold and silver and fancy clothes as a gift, but he didn't want them.

GOD HAD HEALED ME, AND HE DID IT FOR FREE.

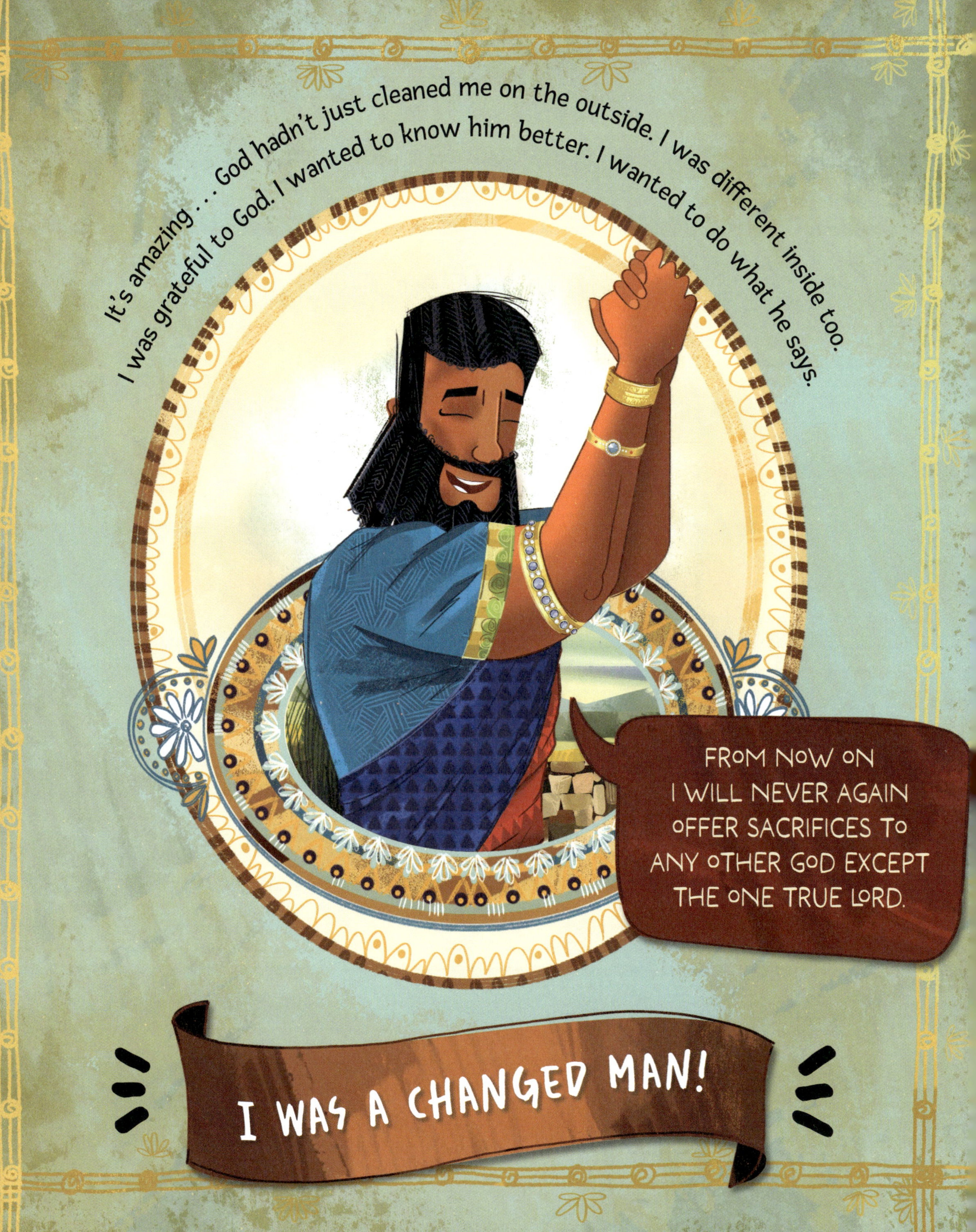
It's amazing . . . God hadn't just cleaned me on the outside. I was different inside too.
I was grateful to God. I wanted to know him better. I wanted to do what he says.
FROM NOW ON I WILL NEVER AGAIN OFFER SACRIFICES TO ANY OTHER GOD EXCEPT THE ONE TRUE LORD.
I WAS A CHANGED MAN!

DO YOU KNOW THAT ALL OF US ARE COVERED IN A DISEASE?
The Bible says we all are dirty and sick with something called SIN.
YUCK! THIS IS WHAT OUR HEARTS LOOK LIKE!
Sin makes our hearts proud,
so we become too stubborn to listen to God.

Instead, we want to do whatever we want—even if it's bad.

So no matter how many times we wash ourselves on the outside,

we need God to clean us up and change us on the inside.

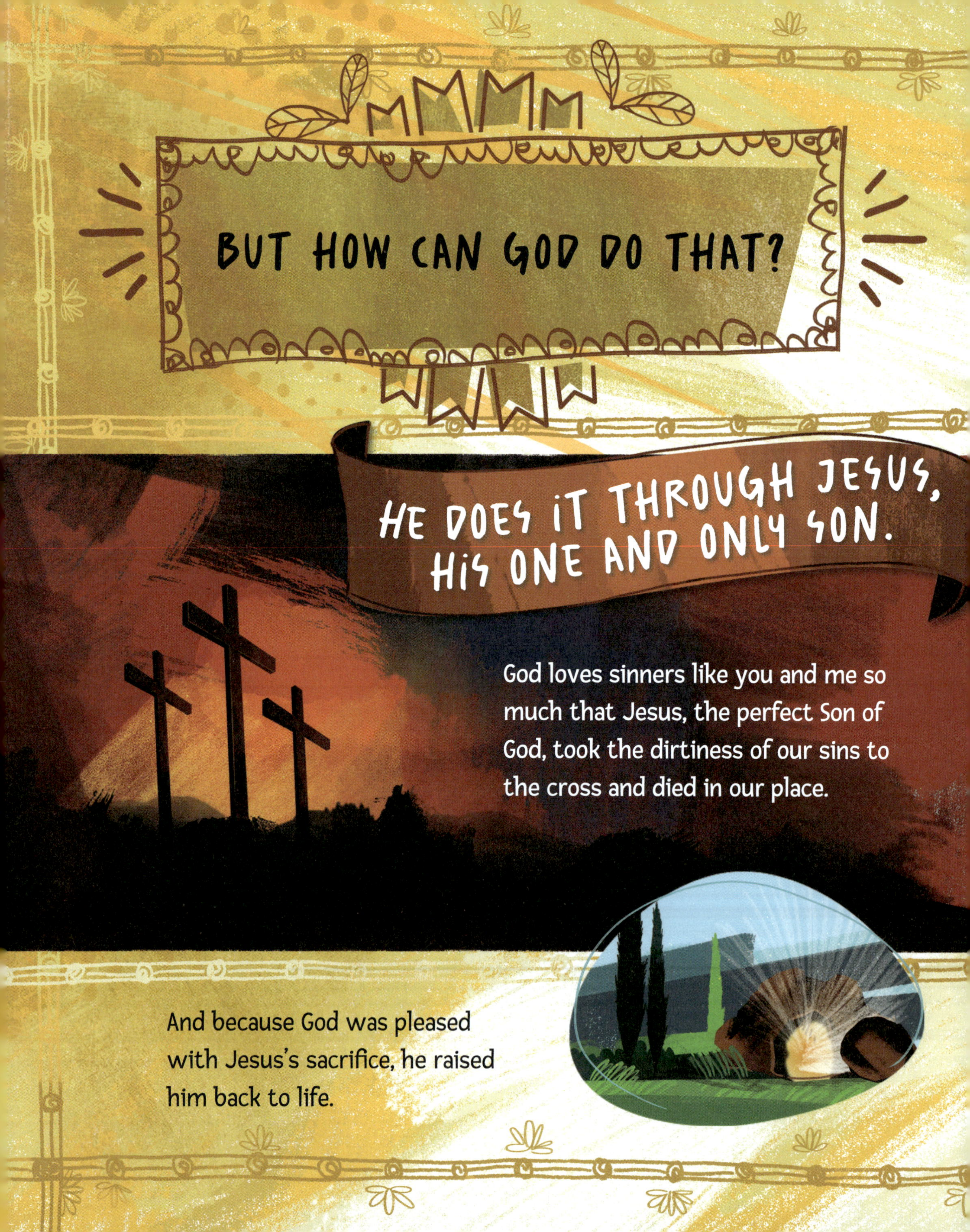

BUT HOW CAN GOD DO THAT?

HE DOES IT THROUGH JESUS, HIS ONE AND ONLY SON.

God loves sinners like you and me so much that Jesus, the perfect Son of God, took the dirtiness of our sins to the cross and died in our place.

And because God was pleased with Jesus's sacrifice, he raised him back to life.

God wants to wash us clean from sin, and change us on the inside, so that we can listen and obey him.

We need grace because—no matter how hard we try—we can never scrub our sins away.

No, you don't need to take a bath in Jesus's blood! You just need to trust in him.
Tell him you don't want your heart to be proud or stubborn anymore.
YES, GOD!
NO, GOD!
YES, GOD!
Tell him you want to do what God wants.
NO, GOD!
WHEN YOU DO, GOD WILL WASH YOU CLEAN FROM YOUR SIN.

That doesn't mean you will never sin again.
But it does mean that sin
will never stick to you like leprosy does.
THE HOLY SPIRIT WILL HELP YOU FOLLOW GOD'S WAY, NOT YOUR WAY, JUST LIKE HE HELPED ME.

BEING HEALED BY GOD WAS
AWESOME!
GOD WASHED AWAY MY LEPROSY!

HE CHANGED ME ON THE INSIDE SO I COULD TRUST HIM!
HE MADE ME ONE OF HIS PEOPLE!
BUT...
DO YOU KNOW THE BEST PART OF ALL?

ONE DAY, WHEN JESUS COMES AGAIN, HE WILL HEAL EVERYTHING.

We'll have brand-new,
perfect bodies!

WE'LL WORSHIP THE ONE TRUE
WITH ALL GOD'S PEOPLE FROM

God's holy Bible tells us the way to be clean. We just need to listen and trust that what God says is true. Are you listening?

In the PICTURES OF GOSPEL GRACE series, we retell lesser-known Bible stories to teach children how God shows his saving grace throughout his Word. Our chief aim is to direct children to the ultimate display of God's love and mercy to sinners—the redemption accomplished by the Lord Jesus Christ.

THE BEST BATH EVER tells the true story of how God healed and redeemed a pagan army commander named Naaman. You can read all about it in 2 Kings 5:1–27. The Bible first introduces Naaman as an attacker and raider of Israel. He won many battles and even took some Israelite children prisoner to be servants, but he could not win the fight against a terrible skin disease, leprosy. Later, a captured girl whom he had taken as a servant introduced God's grace to him when she directed him to Elisha for healing. The prophet told Naaman that God would cure him if he washed in the Jordan, and his subsequent miraculous healing convinced him to both trust and worship God.

This true story is a beautiful picture of an even more wonderful true story found in the New Testament. Jesus, the sinless Son of God, came to earth to show God's love for sinners. He did this by multiplying fish and bread to feed the hungry, opening the eyes of the blind, and making the lame walk again. He even touched and healed lepers, just like Naaman! But most important, he died on the cross for our sins and rose from the dead on the third day. Jesus, who is perfectly clean of sin, can wash every kind of sinner clean with his blood. You can read more in Hebrews 10:19–22 and 1 John 1:5–2:2 about how he cleanses us of sin—and in Revelation 21:1–27 about how he will one day heal and fix *everything*.

FOR PARENTS, GRANDPARENTS, AND TEACHERS

Below is a glossary of some key words along with simple definitions that will help guide your discussion of this book. We encourage you to look up the Scripture passages and read them with the children in your life.

BIBLE. God's Book, his holy Word, given to show us what God is like and to tell us how we can have our sins forgiven and be made new when we trust in Jesus Christ. The Bible always tells us the truth.
Read John 5:24.

FOREVER. Time that never runs out. We are always running out of time, so this is hard to understand. The **Bible** says God has always existed forever (not like us, who had to be born), and when we **repent** and trust in Jesus, we will someday live with him forever.
Read Revelation 22:1–5.

GRACE. A gift we receive that we could never be good enough to deserve or pay back. Because we naturally want to disobey God and stay away from him, we can never wash ourselves clean from sin through our own good works. But God, who loves to show kindness to us, did what we could never do for ourselves: Jesus offered his blood to cleanse us of our sin and gives us new hearts that trust in him.
Read 2 Corinthians 5:21; Ephesians 2:8–10.

IDOL. A false god. God hates idols because he is the only God and the one we should love and serve more than anyone, or anything, else. The **Bible** commands us to turn away from idols and to worship only the true God.
Read Exodus 20:4–5; Psalm 115:1–8; Colossians 3:1–5.

LEPROSY. A skin disease that can cause serious physical damage. In ancient times, infected people had to follow strict rules and stay away from others. Jesus healed many people of their leprosy so that they could live with their friends and family again and worship with the rest of God's people.
Read Leviticus 14:1–32; Luke 17:11–19.

PROPHET. A person God chooses to do and say important things for him. God expected his people to listen to and obey his prophets when they spoke for him, just as they should listen to and obey God himself. God no longer chooses prophets because we have his words written down for us in the **Bible**.
Read Jeremiah 1:4–9; 2 Peter 1:19–21.

REPENT. To turn around and go the other direction, away from doing whatever we want and toward God and his love. God's gift of **grace** helps us understand we are unclean and changes our hearts so that we don't want to disobey God anymore but trust in Jesus as our Savior, King, and Friend.
Read Luke 5:27–32; 2 Peter 3:9.

SACRIFICE. A valuable gift that should be offered to the one true God but is sometimes wrongly offered to **idols** instead. We could never offer the perfect sacrifice to please God, so God sent his Son, Jesus, to be a perfect sacrifice for us. When we trust in Jesus, God makes us new and pleasing to him.
Read Romans 12:1–2; Hebrews 10:1–18.

SINNER. Someone who does not love God or do what he tells them to do because they love themselves and their own way more. The **Bible** teaches that every one of us is a sinner. We are all selfish and stubborn. We refuse to listen to others—even God—or do what we are told. We all deserve to be punished, yet God loved us while we were sinners and sent his Son, Jesus, as a **sacrifice** to take our punishment.
Read Romans 3:23–25; 5:8; 6:23.

When Naaman **listened and obeyed** God's command, he became new—**inside and out!** Sin makes our hearts **dirty and sick**, but when we trust God, he makes them **clean and healthy.**

CAN YOU SPOT OTHER PAIRS IN THIS BOOK?
(Hint: There are three sets of twins!)